J. S. Brazeau

Hand-guide to Montreal:

Containing all necessary information and advice for strangers, including

rates of money, carriage tariff, institutions and other places of interest to

visit - when and how to see them - fancy and fashionable stores, &c

J. S. Brazeau

Hand-guide to Montreal:
Containing all necessary information and advice for strangers, including rates of money, carriage tariff, institutions and other places of interest to visit - when and how to see them - fancy and fashionable stores, &c

ISBN/EAN: 9783337763930

Printed in Europe, USA, Canada, Australia, Japan

Cover: Foto ©ninafisch / pixelio.de

More available books at **www.hansebooks.com**

HAND-GUIDE

TO

MONTREAL

WITH MAP OF THE CITY

*Containing all necessary information and
advice for Strangers, including rates of Money,
Carriage tariff, Institutions and other
places of interest to visit—
when and how to see them—Fancy and
Fashionable Stores, &c.*

PRICE, 25 CENTS.

J. S. BRAZEAU,

Publisher and Proprietor News and Telegraph Office,

ST. LAWRENCE HALL,

MONTREAL.

CONTENTS.

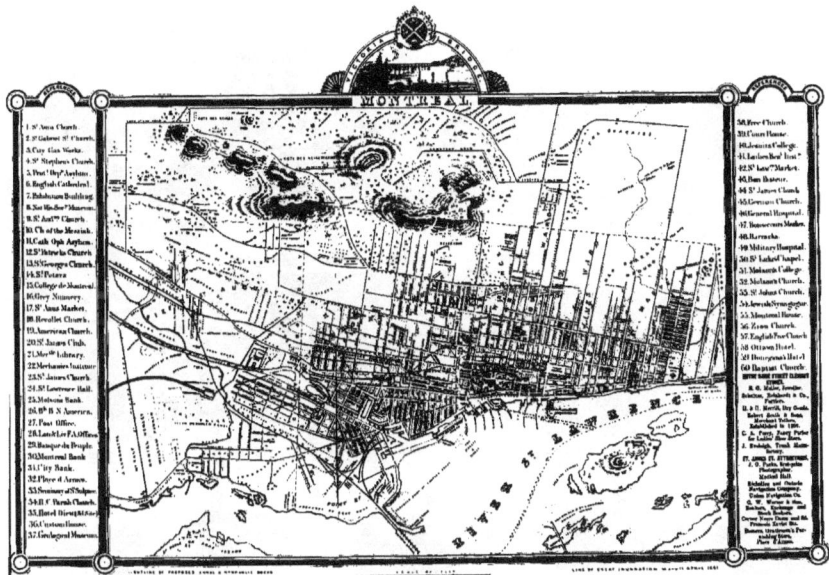

POCKET MAP OF THE CITY OF MONTREAL.

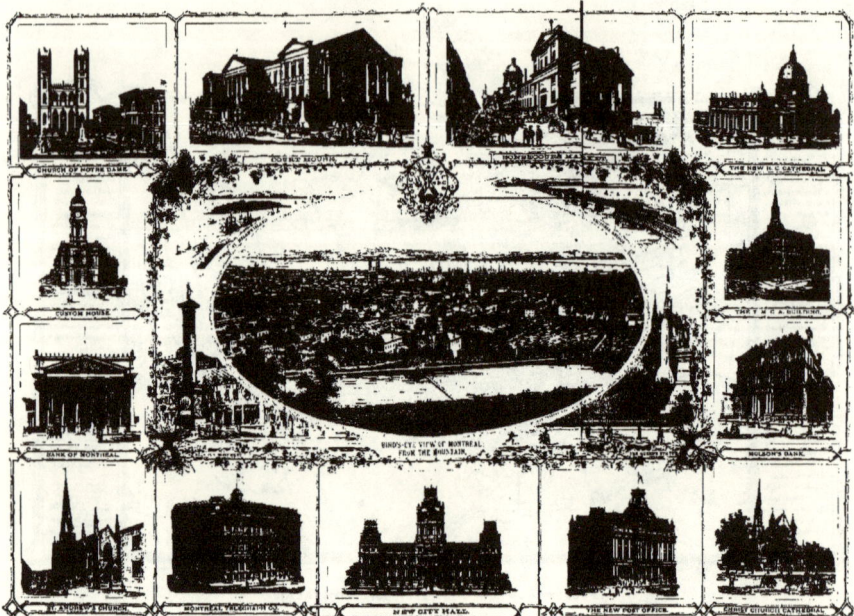

MONTREAL AND ITS PUBLIC BUILDINGS.

291

HATS, CAPS, AND FURS, WHOLESALE AND RETAIL.

291 SCHULTZE, REINHARDT & CO. 291

WALKER & WILLMAN

SCHULTZE, REINHARDT & CO.'S HAT & FUR STORE.

MONTREAL.

It is known that the history of this City dates back to the time when the redman reigned on the banks of the St. Lawrence. It was founded in 1642, not far from the site of the early Indian village of Hochelaga, and its first name was Ville Marie. It subsequently took that of *Mount Royal* from the grand elevation which immediately overlooks it, now so well known as the Mountain. It is situated on the magnificent St. Lawrence, in view of *St. Helen's Island, Isle Ronde, Isle aux Fraises*, Moffatt's Island, and St. Paul's or Nuns' Island, latitude 45°30'21 N., longitude 72°33'30 W. Population of latest census, 160,000 inhabitants. The City Corporation consists of a Mayor and twenty-seven members, designated Aldermen.

The city improvements are rapidly extending, and a large extent of mountain property has been lately secured with a view to constructing a Public Park on a scale and with surroundings which will not be surpassed on

the American Continent. Besides the many
Churches, Convents, Colleges, Charitable Institutions, all of which are referred to in detail
in the following pages, there are several Establishments in this City to visit, which would
well repay the business man, the lover of
science, and the friend of progress. Amongst
those are the City Gaz Works, Water Works,
Gould's extensive Mills, Hudon's Cotton
Factory, Redpath's Sugar Factory, the Natural History Society's Museum, the Mechanics'
Institute, the Mercantile Library, and the
Geological Museum.

The Hotel accommodation may be said to
be respectable in extent and quality, the
principal Establishments being the St. Lawrence Hall, the Ottawa, the Albion and the
Montreal House; but a grand enterprise in
this line has just been announced; active pro-
ceedings have commenced to erect the
Windsor in a fashionable and otherwise most
desirable locality, at the very base of the
Mountain. This building will be in Italian
style, 250 feet square, with a tower on the
Peel and Dorchester Street corner. From the
sidewalk to the top of the balustrade, which
will surmount the roof of the building proper, the height will be 100 feet, and to the
top of the tower 140. The several fronts

will be of cut stone; there will be four hundred rooms, and accommodation for one thousand guests. The dining-room will be on the
second story—dimensions, 132x52 feet;
the ladies' ordinary or dining-room will be
56x42. Leading to the large dining-room
will be a nice passage 112x30, divided by a
row of columns. In this will be an alcove
for a band, and here guests will promenade in
the evening. The rooms are all of good size
and well lighted, a wide court giving light to
the inner rows. There will be a number of
suites of rooms, each furnished with a bath,
wardrobe, &c.; also a stylish bridal suite.
Guests will be conveyed to the different flats
by elevators; but for elderly people and others
who do not care to be located up-stairs, there
will be plenty of rooms on the office-flat. The
Hotel will be heated with steam throughout.
The system of communication will be by
electric bells to an office, whence a clerk
will convey the orders to the several depart-
ments. It is stated on authority that the
appointments of the Windsor will be equal, if
not superior, to any Hotel on the continent;
and that it will be fully completed as early as
June, 1876, at a cost of no less than half a
million of dollars.

In approaching the City of Montreal by

water, the stranger's eye is soon attracted by the long line of cut-stone buildings which fronts the river and which are alike solid and elegant in style; and as he nears the shore, he is also led to admire an extensive range of wharves, built of first-class limestone, and unsurpassed in strength and workmanship by any in America, perhaps in the world.

It would be simply improper to close this sketch without referring to the stupendous VICTORIA BRIDGE, spanning the St. Lawrence from the western extremity of the City. The cost of this tubular wonder was not less than EIGHT MILLIONS of DOLLARS. There are 25,000 tons of stone, and 7,500 tons of iron embedded in it; the contents of its masonry are three millions of cubic feet, and its total length from bank to bank is 10,284 feet, or about 50 yards less than two English miles.

VALUE OF SILVER COINS.

United States Half-Dollar . .		45	cts.
do Quarters .	.	20	"
do Ten Cents . .		8	"
do Five Cents .	.	4	"
British Shillings . . .	.	24	"
do Sixpence		12	"
Canadian Silver at par.			

AN ADVICE TO THE STRANGER.

In arriving into Montreal, the visitor should by all means get the Hand-Guide and Map of the City, in which he will find carters' tariff, and rates of money. Be sure also and get your American paper exchanged for Canadian, as some stores would take that advantage in charging you double for any goods you might purchase. Also, to prevent this, we give you in this book a list of the principal stores where you will be certain to get the value of your money. We advertise none but those we can strongly recommend.

H. & H. MERRILL.

TARIFF FOR HACKNEY CARRIAGES.

PLACES.	Two or four wheeled carriages drawn by one horse.		Coaches or four wheeled carriages drawn by two horses.		TIME ALLOWED.
	For one or two persons.	For three or four persons.	For one or two persons.	For three or four persons.	
	$ cts.	$ cts.	$ cts.	$ cts.	
From any place to any other within the same Division and back.........	0 15	0 25	0 30	0 40	¼ an hour.
	0 25	0 00	0 00	0 00	
From any Division to any place in another Division and back	0 25	0 40	0 40	0 50	¾ of an hour.
	0 35	50	0 60	0 75	{ over ¾ of an hour and under 1 hour.
(Per hour.)					
From any place to any other in the City..............	0 50	0 70	0 75	1 00	One hour.
	0 20	0 30	0 40	0 40	{ For every additional ½ hour.

Reasonable weight of luggage free of charge.

Children under 12 years of age to be charged half-price.

Roman Catholic Institutions and Churches.

PARISH CHURCH OF VILLE-MARIE.

CATHEDRAL OF MONTREAL.

Generally, but improperly, called by British residents the French Cathedral, is, in point of dimensions and area, the pride of Montreal. The great towers seen from afar off bear no inconsiderable resemblance to that of Notre Dame on the banks of the Seine. The corner stone of the edifice, which is built in the perpendicular gothic style of the middle ages, was laid on the 3rd September, 1824, and it was opened for public worship in July, 1829. It was originally intended to make it much larger than it is at present. The height of the towers is 220 feet; the great window at the high altar, which is filled with beautiful stained glass, is 64 feet high and 33 feet wide. The Church is capable of accommodating over seven thousand persons. In the north-east tower is a fine chime of bells, and in the north-west tower is placed the largest bell in America, cast expressly for this Church and weighing 29,400 lbs.; its sound is very remarkable. This tower is open to the public for a small fee; from the top a splendid view of

the River St. Lawrence, the Island of
Montreal, St. Helen's Island, Victoria Bridge,
and the surrounding country, is presented.
This Church is now undergoing great repairs which will not cost less than 50,000
dollars, to make her the finest Church on
the Continent of America.

CHURCH OF THE GESU,

situated on Bleury Street, is in the opi-
nion of many, the most beautiful Church
edifice in America. The style of architecture
is the Round Roman Arch; it is 194 feet long,
and 96 wide, but at the transept the trans-
versal nave is 144 feet long. The height of
the two naves is 75 feet. The Gesu forms a
perfect cross. The head of the cross is
formed by the sanctuary. The interior is frescoed in the most elaborate manner. Over the
high altar is a beautiful fresco representing
the Crucifixion of Our Lord. Higher up the
center piece is a scene from the Apocalypse.
On the ceiling of the sanctuary the shepherds
are seen adoring the new-born Savior. There
are also in the Church several very fine
paintings. The Church of the Gesu is
attached to St. Mary's College, and both be-
long to the Jesuit Fathers.

ST. PATRICK'S CHURCH

stands on an elevated site at the corner of St. Alexander and Lagauchetière Streets, and is one of the most striking objects visible on approaching the City. This large and commanding building is in gothic style of architecture; the length is 240 feet by 90 feet in breadth; the spire is 225 feet high. The interior is comfortably and handsomely fitted up, with room for over 5000 worshippers. Taken altogether, this is a splendid model of ecclesiastical architecture.

ST. ANN'S CHURCH,

on McCord Street, at the junction with Basin Street, is a handsome stone building in the gothic style of architecture, and will seat about 1,500 persons.

ST. JAMES' CHURCH.

This handsome building is situated on St. Denis Street. Erected upon the ruins of the one destroyed by the fire of 1852, known as the Bishop's Church, which was of the Roman Ionic style, but altered in form and extended in length, is now built after the most admired specimens of the early pointed style; it is a fine example of what is sometimes called Christian architecture. The windows are of stained glass.

THE CANADIAN ST. PETER.

There is now in course of erection a Cathedral unequalled on the Continent, for size and imposing appearance.   In 1852, the old Cathedral and Episcopal Palace which for so long had stood on St. Denis Street, were destroyed by fire.   Shortly after, a Parish Church was built on the old site in the East End, and the Bishop's removed to new and roomy quarters in the large and plain-looking brick mansion on Palace Street, which he now occupies. A few years later, by the purchase of a portion of the estate of the late Jacob de Witt, and a section of ground from the Fabrique of the Parish of Notre Dame, used as a cemetery, Bishop Bourget had under control a large block of land in an elevated position, situated in the West End, adjoining his Palace, and very suitable for the erection of a giant Cathedral. He shaped his plans accordingly and the Catholics in his diocese, gradually becoming wealthy, afforded him an opportunity to indulge in the ambitious project of building an edifice which would rival the New York Cathedral in size and magnificence and surpass all others in America. The Cathedral is being erected in the form of a cross, 300 feet in length from the grand entrance to the back of the nave, while its breadth, or length of the transept, is 225 feet. The length of the building will be further increased by a portico 30 feet in width. The average height of the walls will be 30 feet. Those to support the roof of the nave will have to go forty feet higher, with an additional elevation of 66 feet under the great dome. Thus the extreme height of the masonry from the floor will be 138 feet. The roof, which is to be of galvanised iron, will not be modelled after that of St. Peter's, for though at Rome the climate admits of a flat roof, it is otherwise in Canada. The large dome will be the handsomest part of the Cathedral; it will be an exact copy on a smaller scale of the mighty dome of St. Peter's, and when completed will be 250 in height, 46 feet higher than the towers of the French Church in the Place d'Armes. The front entrance will be on Dorchester Street, and there will be no colonade by which to approach the edifice, as at St. Peter's, Rome ; but the grounds are to be ornamented with fountains, &c.

NOTRE DAME DE LOURDES.

This fine and new Church, not yet completed, is situated on St. Catherine Street, in the east part of the City.   It is also an ornament to the many Catholic institutions, and no visitor should fail to visit this fine edifice.

PROTESTANT CHURCHES.

CHRIST'S CHURCH CATHEDRAL

is situated on St. Catherine Street, corner of University; is a beautiful edifice in the Mediæval gothic style.   The plan is cruciform, and is indeed a model of ecclesiastical style.   The tower and spire, the latter of which is well proportioned and springs gracefully from the former, are the intersection of the four arms of the cross, and measure 224 feet in height.   The Church is built of Caen stone and Montreal limestone.   Length of building inside, 187 feet; width of nave 70 feet ; transept including tower, 99 feet.   The upper stage of the tower contains a peal of bells, and the clocks are placed immediately above the corbel-table.   The windows are

good and copied from the best Mediæval English Churches. The front entrance is beautifully designed; in fact the building is unequalled on this Continent.

ST. GEORGE'S CHURCH (EPISCOPAL)

is situated on St. François de Salles and St. Janvier Streets. The material of the building is Montreal stone. The massive gothic entrance, attractive and beautiful, though without any profusion of ornament, with the modest symbols of Church and Crown, strong in their inherent right, is an excellent vestibule to a Church which bears the same of England's Patron Saint. The window tracery and chancel decoration are very tasteful. The transepts are 45 feet in length by 24 feet deep ; the chancel and choir together are 40 feet deep. The gas pendants are of singularly beautiful workmanship; there are ten, five on each side, beside the one in front of the chancel. The utmost intelligence and foresight have been expended on every detail of this fine church.

TRINITY CHURCH (EPISCOPAL)

is a very elegant building situated on the north-west corner of Viger Square and St.

Denis Street; is of the early English Gothic style of architecture, and is built entirely of Montreal stone. The building is 167 feet in length, by 76 in breadth, including the tower and chancel. Total height of tower and spire, 168 feet. The church will seat 1,250.

There are more Episcopal Churches: the St. Thomas', on St. Mary Street; St. Stephens, Dalhousie Street; St. Luke, Dorchester Street; Church of St. James the Apostle, St. Catherine Street; Church of St. John the Evangelist, Dorchester Stteet; St. Mary's Church, Hochelaga.

AMERICAN BRESBYTERIAN CHURCH,

on Dorchester Street, built in 1855-6; is an exact copy of Park Church in Brooklyn, N.Y. Its length is 144 feet, and the width 86 feet. Has two towers, one being finished with a spire rising 200 feet above the street. Will seat 1,200.

ST. ANDREW'S (CHURCH OF SCOTLAND),

built in 1850, on Beaver Hall Hill. The building is of Montreal stone, with a tower and spire 180 feet high.

Interior dimensions, 90 feet by 65 feet.

Will seat about 1000. Was destroyed by fier in 1869, but rebuilt according to the original plan.

The other Presbyterian Churches are Knox Church, Dorchester Street ; St. Gabriel Street Church ; St. Paul and Erskine Churches, the latter on Dorchester Street.

WESLEYAN METHODIST CHURCH

is situated on St. James Street. This is the largest Wesleyan Church in the city. It is an elegant building of the Florid Gothic style; its size is 111 feet by 73 feet. Will comfortably seat 2,500 persons; it contains a splendid organ. The windows (several of which are memorial windows) are filled with stained glass of most elaborate design.

FRENCH EVANGELICAL CHURCH

is situated on the corner of Craig and St. Elizabeth Streets, and is under under the direction of the French Canadian Missionary Society. It is a handsome stone edifice of the Gothic order; will seat about 300 persons.

FRENCH PROTESTANT CHURCH,

on Dorchester Street, is a plain, neat brick building in Gothic style; will seat 300.

ZION CHURCH (Congregational)

is situated on Beaver Hall Hill. Was built in 1846; is of the Doric order of architecture, and will seat about 1,400 persons. In 1868 the organ roof and tower were destroyed by fire ; repairs were completed in May, 1869.

ST. JOHN'S CHURCH (German Protestant),

on St. Dominique Street, was erected in 1858. Cost $7,000.

NEW JERUSALEM CHURCH (Sweedenborgian)

is situated on Dorchester Street, corner of Hanover.

THE SHERBROOKE STREET CHURCH (Wesleyan.)

This building is entirely of Montreal stone. Cost about $20,000. On the front is a tower and spire, rising to the height of 120 feet. Will seat about 500.

THE OTTAWA STREET CHURCH (Wesleyan)

Was opened for public worship in 1846. It is 60 feet by 85 feet, and will accommodate 1000 persons.

DORCHESTER STREET CHURCH (Wesleyan).

The style of architecture is English Gothic of the 13th century ; it is 63 feet by 93 feet inside ; will accommodate 800 persons ; will seat about 500.

THE NEW CONNEXION METHODIST

have two churches known as Salem and Ebenezer Chapels; the first is situated on Panet Street, and the latter in Dupre Lane.

BAPTIST CHURCH,

Beaver Hall Hill, was opened for public worship in 1862. It is the early English Gothic style, surmounted by a tower, and is built entirely of stone. The edifice is 55 feet wide and 80 feet in depth. The front and rear windows are adorned with stained glass, filled in with religious emblems and mottoes Cost of the church ·about $50,000. Will accommodate about 1,000.

CHURCH OF THE MESSIAH (Unitarian)

is situated on Beaver Hall Hill. The style of architecture is the Bizantine. Accommodation is offered for 800 persons.

SYNAGOGUES.

There are only two, one on Chenneville Street, occupied by the English-speaking Jews, and the other on St. Constant Street, occupied by the German Jews.

CHARITABLE INSTITUTIONS.

THE HOTEL-DIEU.

This is the most extensive religious edifice in America; it is composed of the Church, Convent and Hospital. The grounds are surrounded by a massive stone wall, the circumference of which is one and a half mile. The physicians of the institution are the Professors of the French School of Medicine. Previous to the conquest, the Hotel-Dieu was supplied with medicines and other necessaries by the French government; at present the funds are derived from rents of lands, charitable bequests or donations, and an annual grant from Parliament.

THE GREY NUNNERY,

also called Montreal General Hospital, is
situated on St. Catherine Street west. Of
the size of the institution, we may form an
idea from the fact that at present it contains
139 nuns, known as Sisters of Charity, 37
novices, and 500 inmates, while over 5,000
visits are made annually to the sick and poor
of the city, and from the dispensary over
10,000 prescriptions are given to the poor,
gratis, during each year. In addition to
their own establishment, and the visits of
the sick, the Sisters have under their charge
several other benevolent institutions, viz.:

St. Joseph Asylum, on Cemetery Street,
for the reception of orphan boys and girls,
which has 250 inmates;

St. Patrick's Asylum, connected with the
St. Patrick's Church, which contains about
200 inmates. It was founded in 1849, solely
for Irish orphans and aged persons. In connection with this asylum is an infant school,
also taught by the Sisters, which is attended
by 450 pupils;

Nazareth Asylum, for the blind and infant
school; is built on St. Catherine Street; has
over 425 pupils and a number of blind
persons.

PROTESTANT INSTITUTIONS.

MONTREAL PROTESTANT ORPHAN ASYLUM,

situated on St. Catherine Street, is a stone building of neat appearance, and has pleasant grounds attached. Children are not allowed to leave the Asylum before the age of 8 or 9 years, except when adopted into respectable families. The orphans are instructed in the rudiments of a religious and useful English education ; and the girls in addition to needle work, are early taught the domestic duties of the establishment. There are also in the city upwards of 60 societies, such as the German, New England, Irish Protestant Benevolent, St. Patrick's, St. George's, St. Andrew's, &c., &c., which afford to their members, or others, relief, assistance or protection.

PROTESTANT HOUSE OF INDUSTRY & REFUGE

is situated on Dorchester Street, near Bleury. The building is of brick, three stories in height, with basement. On the first story is the ladies' industrial department, and the general offices of the institution ; the second story contains the Board-room and dwelling of the superintendent; the third story being fitted up as dormitories. Religious services are conducted in the Board-room, every Sabbath afternoon, by the clergymen of the city in turn.

THE PLEASANT DRIVES.

The drive around the mountain is certainly one of which it would be difficult, for natural beauty, to surpass. On a clear, bright day, the view from any point of the drive is magnificent; several hundred feet below is spread out a gorgeous panorama of ever-varying beauty, affording commanding and attractive views of the Canadian metropolis, and the great river of the North. Well stocked and highly cultivated farms attest the prosperity of the husbandman; comfortable homesteads, nestling 'mid a luxurious growth, dot the landscape; here and there broad belts of forest shade the view, and form a fringework to the picture; looming up faintly shadowed in the distance, the far off hills of Vermont rear their summit, while like a silver thread winding through the valley, the majestic St. Lawrence flows onward to the sea, spanned at this point by the Victoria Bridge, one of the greatest modern specimens of engineering skill. Handsome private dwellings, faced with gardens laid out with great taste, line the roadway and add to the beauty of the scene.

TO LACHINE.

The drive to Lachine (9 miles) is one of the greatest interest. Lachine is the summer residence of many Montrealers, and becomes famous by its annual regattas. It is noted as being the scene of a terrible massacre of the whites by the Iroquois Indians, in the year 1669, when over two hundred persons were burned alive. Gaughnawaga, an Indian village, is situated immediately opposite, and is connected by a steam ferry.

The Lachine road leads along the bank of St. Lawrence and commands views of scenery of unsurpassed beauty and grandeur.

TO LONGUE POINTE.

Another favorite drive is in an opposite direction to the last, to Longue Pointe, pass-

ing through the village of Hochelaga. The
river scenery in this direction is very fine,
and of quite a different character from that
west of the city. The villages of Longueuil,
Boucherville and Varennes may be seen on
the opposite side of the river.

THE LACHINE RAPIDS.

One of the most delightful, as well as most
exciting experiences of the visitor to Montreal,
is the descent of the Lachine Rapids. A
train leaves Bonaventure Station every morn-
ing at 7 o'clock for Lachine (9 miles), where
a staunch steamer is in readiness, on which
passengers may embark and return to the
city ; shooting the Rapids, and passing
under Victoria Bridge on the way. This
little trip should on no account be omitted
from the tourist's programme.

The time consumed is but little more than
two hours, but the sensations of those two
hours are such as will not be forgotten
during a lifetime.

The following description of the descent of
the Rapids, taken from an American news-
paper, will be found interesting : " Here a
boat came off from the village (the Indian

PERRY'S

Parlor Boot & Shoe Store,

No. 375

NOTRE DAME STREET.

E. & A. PERRY,

(Late of BURT'S, Brooklyn.)

village of Caughnawaga) and brings an Indian.
He is a fine-looking man, apparently about
60 years of age ; he came on board to pilot
the boat over the Lachine, which is the last
but the most dangerous of the rapids. As
the boat moves onward to the rapids, all the
passengers are anxious to get a good position,
in order to have a good view of the heaving,
breaking and laughing waters. As we near
the rapids, we appear to be running upon a
small grass-crowned rocky island. Indeed
the bow of the boat is so near that it appears
to be impossible to clear it ; we look to see if
the pilot is at the helm. Yes, there he stands,
the captain at his post in front of the wheel-
house, and the Indian pilot with three other
strong men at the wheel ; and as we look at
the calm countenance of the Indian, and see
that his bright eye does not so much as
wink, but is fixed steadily upon his beacon,
whatever it may be, and the wheels-men are
fully under his control, we feel that, with
his skill, care and knowledge of the way, we
may banish fear from our thoughts. He guides
the boat among the islands and rocks, over
the rapids and through the intricate channels
as easily as a skilful horseman reins a high
spirited charger. As quick as thought the
boat glides away from these rocks, which it

appears impossible to avoid, but the pilot apparently is insensible to fear, though not to the responsibility that rests upon him. He is aware, and all are aware, that one false move and all is lost : for the current is so swift, the seas run so high, and the boat is driven so rapidly, that one touch upon a rock would shiver her to atoms. Although the passage of the rapids appears to be so dangerous, a sense of pleasure and excitement takes the place of fear."

THE VICTORIA BRIDGE.

The Victoria Bridge (built under the superintendence of the celebrated Robert Stephenson), the longest and largest bridge in the world, is that known as the tubular or beam bridge, and consists of a series of iron tubes resting on 24 stone piers, with a distance between each pier of 242 feet, except the centre opening, which is 330 feet in length. Its total length between the abutments is 6,600 feet, or a mile and a quarter. The bridge is approached by massive embankments, the one on the Montreal side being 1,200 feet, and that on the south shore 800 feet in length, which together, including the abutments, makes the total length of the bridge 9,084 feet, or nearly a mile and three-quarters.

The cost of this gigantic structure was $6,300,000. In its erection 250,000 tons of stone, and 8,000 tons of iron have been used.

The following are the dimensions of the tube through which the trains pass, viz.: in the middle span, 22 feet high, 16 feet wide; at the extreme end, 19 feet high, 16 feet wide; the height above summer water level in the centre opening is 60 feet, decending to either end at the rate of one in 130.

The foundation stone was laid on the 22nd July, 1854, and the bridge was completed in 1860. It is used only for railway transit. No train is allowed to enter the bridge without a written permit from the proper officer, thus insuring exemption of collision or accident; the passage occupies about six minutes, though seeming much longer to the passenger, as it is somewhat cheerless. The river beneath the bridge has a swift current, and the piers are calculated to withstand immense pressure from descending masses of ice.

NELSON'S MONUMENT.

This ornament, erected in the memory of the hero of Trafalgar, stands in Jacques

Cartier Square. The foundation was laid on the 17th of August, 1808.

OUR ELEGANT STORES.

SCHULTZE, REINHARDT & CO.,

First Prize Furriers, 291 Notre Dame Street. It will well repay the tourist to pay a visit to their fine show-rooms of Indian Curiosities and rich Russian Furs, &c.

E. G. MELLOR,

Jeweller, 285 Notre Dame Street, importer of Genuine Gold Jewellery. No visitor should fail in paying this elegant palace a visit.

H. & H. MERRILL,

Dry Goods, Notre Dame Street. This is the pride of Montreal stores, for Silks, Laces, &c.

PUBLIC SQUARES AND GARDEN.

At the head of McGill Street, the Victoria Square is neatly laid out, the centre being occupied by a large fountain. Being comparatively a new square, the trees are yet but small. At the south end of the square is placed the beautiful bronze statue of Queen Victoria. This work of art is from the studio of Mr. Marshall Wood, and was presented to the city by H. E. the Governor General on the 21st November, 1872. The cost of the statue was about $3,000, together with the pedestal, the latter the gift of the Corporation.

VIGER SQUARE OR GARDEN

is situated on Craig and St. Denis Streets. It contains three fountains, the largest one being in the centre of the square. Close by this fountain is a neat conservatory for the propagation of flowering roots, etc., for the decoration of this and other city squares. The grounds are beautifully laid out, and the utmost care and great discremination has been displayed in the choice of trees and shrubs, which are plentifully cultivated.

CHAMP DE MARS.

This spot, now the property of the Dominion Government, was formerly held by the Imperial Government, and used by them as a parade, or drill ground, for the use of the troops. It is 240 yards long by 120 wide, and is perfectly level. On the embankment, next to Notre Dame Street, a range of stairs extends along the whole length of the parade for accommodation of citizens during the public reviews, &c.; along the upper part of the stairs is a broad terrace which serves as an agreeable promenade. It is situated immediately in rear of the Court House.

MOUNT ROYAL PARK.

The city has recently acquired a large property on the slope of the Mountain, for the use of the citizens as a public Park, which for beauty and variety, for its accessibility to the city, for size, and for the magnificence of the prospect which it commands, stands unrivalled in the world.

PUBLIC BUILDINGS.

THE COURT HOUSE.

This building, situated on Notre Dame Street, is after the Grecian style of architecture, and is in its unpretending and massive grandeur, second to few buildings in the city. Ths most striking feature is its large Ionic portico and the bold projection of the pediment, which gives the central portion of the principal front a very noble appearance. There is now in course of erection a new Court House, which will be called City Hall and which, it is said, will be the finest building in Montreal, perhaps in America.

CUSTOM HOUSE.

The new Custom House is the splendid building erected by the Royal Canadian Insurance Company, and which the Government, in 1870, purchased for $200,000; the splendid oak furniture and fittings, safes, &c., being transferred with the property. Alterations were made to make it suitable for its new purposes. There are three principal en-

trances, one, and the most imposing, being
that by the stone portico, facing on Custom
House Square, and the other two being from
Commissionners Street, and Common Street
respectively. Entering by this main entrance
the landing-waiter offices are on the left hand
side, and the warehouse offices on the right.
Immediately adjoining the former is the sur-
veyors' offices. Passing through the landing-
waiters' room, we come to the offices of the
sampler and weigher, and the tide-surveyor.
The first offices on the second story are those
of the collector, a large room for the clerks
and which may be used as a waiting-room;
adjoining it the public offices of the collector,
and again adjoining this a private office, all
of them neatly fitted up. The warehousing
assortments are exceedingly spacious and
commodious. Three elevators worked by
steam power are used in taking packages to
the different flats.

BONSECOURS MARKET

is equal, if not superior, to any building of
the kind in America. It is of the Grecian
Doric style of architecture; the cost of its
erection was about $200,000. One half of the

upper portion of this building is occupied by the offices of the Corporation and the Council chamber. This building is the first to attract the attention of the tourist as he approaches the city from the river. It has an extensive frontage on the river side and is three stories in height, with a lofty dome.

MERCHANTS' EXCHANGE.

This building is three stories high, with basement and finished attics. The ground floor is divided into large double offices, with safes. On the second floor is the reading-room sixty feet by thirty-two feet, extending from front to rear, with offices for the secretary and two other double offices. The third and fourth are occupied as offices, a portion of the latter being used as a residence for the keeper. The building is heated with steam. the facades are cut stone, the principal one, facing on St. Sacrament Street, being in the Italian style, with main entrance in the centre.

CORN EXCHANGE.

This building forms the corner of St. Sacrament, St. John and St. Alexis Streets.

It is three stories in height, the upper one
being equal in height to the two lower ones.
The lower story and a portion of the second
is of dressed Montreal stone. The upper
portion is of red brick, with stone dressing.
The upper flat is fitted up as an elegant and
spacious Hall for the transaction of business ;
and is frescoed in a simple and yet effective
style.   The room is well lighted with lofty
windows on three sides. Adjoining this room
is the Secretary's office and Board-room.

MECHANICS' INSTITUTE,

corner St. James and St. Peter Streets, is in
the Italian style of architecture, and consists
of three divisions ; the centre having a portico with columns and rusticated pillars on
lower story.   The pillars and quoins are
ornamented. In the second story is the reading-room, which is supplied with all the leading newspapers and periodicals.

INSTITUT CANADIEN.

This institution occupies and owns a building of cut stone, four stories in height,
situated on Notre Dame Street. It was

founded 1844, previous to which the French had not a single library in the city, nor a place where they could read, or meet together. It was incorporated in 1852.

There are several other public libraries in Montreal, as follows: Advocate's Library and Library of the Bar, founded 1827; Canadian Mechanics' Institute, founded 1857; Grand Trunk Reading Room and Library; Institut Canadien Français; Œuvre des Bons Livres, founded in 1844.

NATURAL HISTORY SOCIETY'S MUSEUM

is situated on University Street, and is built of white brick. On the ground floor is the lecture-room, library, committee-room, and residence of the keeper. The second story, which is about 36 feet in height, contains the museum, which is surrounded by a gallery, and lighted by skylights. Around the sides of the principal hall are cases containing birds, reptiles and quadrupeds. The centre is occupied by cases of mineralogical and geological specimens. In the galleries are specimens of shell fish, corals and shells, of which a large collection of fine specimens are exhibited. The walls are hung with paintings,

Indian dresses and curiosities, specimens of
paper money, cases of coins, medals, &c.
The principal attraction in the galleries is the
Ferrier collection of Egyptian and other
antiquities, collected by Hon. James Ferrier
during a tour in the East, and presented to
the Society by him.

GEOLOGICAL SURVEY'S MUSEUM,

situated opposite the west end of Champ
de Mars, is a plain stone edifice, three stories
in height. It is open from 10 a.m. to 4 p.m.,
and is free to all.

THE NEW POST OFFICE

now in course of erection on the corner of
St. James and St. Francois Xavier Streets,
has a frontage on St. James Street of 120 feet,
and its depth from St. Francois Xavier Street
to the Montreal Bank building will be 95
feet. The height of the main building from
ground level to the roof will be 88 feet, and
from the basement to summit of central tower
will be 120 feet. The building is constructed of Montreal grey stone. The style
of architecture is the modern Italian. The

facade on St. James Street is highly ornamented with cut stone pillars, pediments
and carved portico, while the mansard roof
is decorated with richly furnished mould-
ings. The central tower is to contain a large
illuminated clock with immense dial plate.
The mansard roof will be of wood and pro-
tected with iron and slates. The basement
and first floor will be constructed of fire-proof
materials, and the entire frame of the building is to be of iron, while the floors will be
laid of Baccerini cement, and well traversed
with iron for preservation of the valuable
contents of the building. It will cost about
$500,000.

VICTORIA SKATING RINK.

Skating is one of the most popular of the
amusements pursued by the citizens of Montreal during the winter season. While the
river St. Lawrence furnishes room for all who
may desire to practice the art, still the violent
storms often prevent its being practiced in
exposed places.
The provide against this, several private
rinks have been erected, the principal one
being that known as the Victoria Rink.
The building is 250 feet long by 100

broad, is built of brick and covered by a semi-circular arch-like roof fifty feet high in the centre. The space used for skating is surrounded by a promenade, raised about a foot above the level of the ice. The front portion of the building is two stories in height, and contains on the lower floor, commodious dressing and cloak rooms and offices.

YOUNG MEN'S CHRISTIAN ASSOCIATION BUILDING.

This building, situated on the corner of Craig and Radegonde Streets, is one of the finest in the City; it contains a reading-room which is free to all, and is a most elegant and cheerful apartment.

DOMINION TELEGRAPH COMPANY

is situated on St. François Xavier Street. This Company has connection with all places in United States and Canada, and will soon connect with European lines.

C. R. HOSMER, Superintendent.

S. E. GARVEY, Gl. Manager.

BANK BUILDINGS.

MERCHANTS BANK OF CANADA.

This magnificent edifice, said to be the finest building for commercial purposes in America, is situated on the corner of St. James and St. Peter Streets.

BANK OF MONTREAL, Place d'Armes.

This magnificent building is situated on St. James Street, next to the new Post Office, and its Corinthian style of architecture is perfectly gorgeous. The entrance is by a portico supported by immense columns of cutstone. These are surmounted by a pediment. The sculpture on the pediment is 52 feet long and weighs over twenty-five tons, there being twenty different pieces. The figures are colossal, eight feet in height for a human figure, and are placed at an elevation of fifty feet from the ground. The arms of the Bank, with the motto " *Concordia Salus*," forms the centre of the group ; on each side, *vis-à-vis*, is seated a North American indian. The other two figures are a settler and a sailor on either side, the former, with a calumet or pipe of peace in his hand, reclining upon logs, and surrounded by the implements and emblems of industry, the spade, the plough, the locomotive engine ; literature and music putting in a modest appearance in the distance, in the shape of a book and a lyre. The whole sculpture is in Binny stone. The work was executed by Mr. John Steel, R. S. A., Her Majesty's sculptor in Scotland.

MOLSONS BANK,

situated on the corner of St. James and St. Peter Streets, is a magnificent building; built entirely of Ohio sandstone. It is three stories in height with a lofty basement. The style of architecture is Italian, and is highly ornamented.

BANK OF BRITISH NORTH AMERICA,

situated on St. James Street, near St. François Xavier, is built entirely of cut stone, and is of the composite style of architecture. The head office of this Bank is in London, England. It was established in 1836, and was incorporated by Royal charter in 1840.

ONTARIO BANK

is situated on Place d'Armes. Is in the Italian style of architecture, four stories in height and built of Montreal limestone.

MECHANICS BANK

is a plain three-stories brick building, covered with cement and painted to imitate brown free stone. The banking offices are on the ground floor.

BANQUE JACQUES CARTIER.

The new building occupied by this Bank is situated on the east side of Place d'Armes, and is a well executed building in the modern French Renaissance style, four stories in height, with high mansard roof.

CITY BANK,

on Place d'Armes, is a plain, substantial stone building of the Doric order of architecture.

BANQUE DU PEUPLE

is situated on St. James Street. It is a large building of cut stone, and is three stories in height. Above the windows of the lower story are four compartments, in which are placed emblems representing agriculture, manufactures, arts and commerce, executed in bas-relief.

In addition to those described, the following Banks have their head-offices in this city :

City and District Savings Bank, corner of St. James and St. John Streets.

Metropolitan Bank, Great St. James Street.

Exchange Bank of Canada, 60 St. Francois Xavier Street; and La Banque Ville-Marie, 8 St. Lambert Hill.

ST. LOUIS HOTEL,

ST. LOUIS STREET, QUEBEC.

This Hotel, which is unrivalled for size, style and locality in Quebec, is open throughout the year for pleasure and business travellers. It is eligibly situated in the immediate vicinity of the most delightful and fashionable promenades, —the Governor's Garden, the Citadel, the Esplanade, the Place d'Armes, and Durham Terrace — which furnish the splendid views and magnificent scenery for which Quebec is so justly celebrated, and which are unsurpassed in any part of the world.

The proprietors, in returning thanks for the very liberal patronage they have hitherto enjoyed, inform the public that this Hotel has been thoroughly renovated and embellished, and can now accommodate about 500 visitors ; and assure them that nothing will be wanting on their part that will conduce to the comfort and enjoyment of their guests.

WILLIS RUSSELL & SON,

Proprietors.

G. W. WARNER & SON,

BANKERS,

Exchange & Stock Brokers,

Corner Notre Dame

AND

ST. FRANCOIS XAVIER STREETS,

Near the French Church.

This firm has been existing for over twenty-five years, and known as the most reliable in Montreal.

www.ingramcontent.com/pod-product-compliance
Lightning Source LLC
Chambersburg PA
CBHW031751090426
42739CB00008B/972